# Music while drowning

# Music while drowning

German Expressionist Poems

*Edited by David Miller and Stephen Watts*

Tate Publishing

First published 2003 by order of the Tate Trustees
by Tate Publishing, a division of Tate Enterprises Ltd,
Millbank, London SW1P 4RG www.tate.org.uk

© Tate 2003

British Library Cataloguing in Publication Data
A catalogue record for this book is available from the
British Library

ISBN 1-85437-471-0

Distributed in the United States and Canada by
Harry N. Abrams, Inc., New York

Library of Congress Cataloging in Publication Data
Library of Congress Control Number: 2003100456

Designed and typeset by Anne Odling-Smee
Printed by Snoeck-Ducaju & Zoon, Gent, Belgium

# Contents

### German Expressionist Poetry

*Premises and Context*

The first important anthology of German Expressionist poetry was that by Kurt Pinthus in 1920. He gave it the title *Menschheitsdämmerung*, which, because of the ambiguity of the word 'Dämmerung', might mean either the dawn or the dusk of humanity. The latter, more likely; and not so much a long twilight as an apocalyptic crash. But those contradictory possibilities – the hopeful broaching of a new century or the frightful endgame of a doomed species – do constitute an essential dynamism of German Expressionism.

The philosophical premises of the new century were set by Nietzsche. The writers grew up reading him; or, if they did not read him, they took as a given fact the rubble-heap of values that was his bequest. Nietzsche – or we should say Darwin, Marx and Nietzsche, the three great evolutionists and relativisers of values – had between them demolished the transcendental buttresses and arches of humanity's belief-systems. Values were revealed to be 'Zweck-Hypothesen', hypotheses we devise for the purposes and support of our own class, caste and creed; entirely relative, having to do with the maintenance of quite particular power bases. The century opened in nihilism. As Nietzsche put it: 'Are we not wandering at a loss through an infinite nothingness? Do we not feel the breath of empty space? Has it not become colder? Are we not faced by the oncoming night and yet more night?' But in Nietzsche, as in Marx, the relativisation of all values is also a very liberating and energising thing: all the energy previously going to waste through a hole in the sky can now be directed earthwards, into the existential needs of the individual or of the up-and-coming hitherto enslaved and deluded masses. So the premises are ambivalent:

they give us *tabula rasa*, and they incite us to assert our energies in the one life here and now.

The social context and premises of Expressionism cannot be separated from the philosophical, human consciousness in any period being largely determined by the contemporary material base. The times were urgent, the social forces working in them seemed to many unprecedentedly novel and violent. It was said that in the first two decades of the new century more was visited upon humanity – more 'progress' – than in the previous two millennia. Germany industrialised late, but then colossally, at breakneck speed, with a vengeance; between 1870 and 1913 productive capacity increased eightfold. Much Expressionist poetry comes out of the experience of the big city, and no wonder. Berlin grew from 800,000 inhabitants in 1870 to more than four million by 1920. In the giant new industries of coal and steel, electrics and chemicals, Capitalism boomed and slumped according to laws beyond the comprehension and control of the humans who had created it. Systems became autonomous, their people reduced to cogs and commodities. Everything accelerated: transport, communications, the pace of living. Humankind seemed subjected to a process of 'forcing'; and yet it could not keep up with its own creations, the systems running ahead or running amok. Dislocation, bewilderment and alienation were the air the city-dwellers breathed. Efforts to order the chaos easily resulted in another evil: the reduction of all human relations to the rationalistic criteria of management for maximum profit. Expressionism was largely the forced, hectic and often desperate attempt to deal with a Modernity that had arrived too fast. There was nostalgic harking back to the stability and human closeness of rural community; or a determined and often wildly enthusiastic aiming forwards to the humane re-ordering of Modernity under Socialism. And there was also a sort of riotous Dionysian delight in what threatened or promised to be the end of the world and the species. There was much gaiety in the period, but of a nervous, febrile, almost vindictively brash and violent kind. The social forces, on the surge of which the new citizens danced their dance of death, were immeasurably vast. Capitalism, being as many thought intrinsically competitive and belligerent, went naturally and inevitably over into the War; out of the War came revolution, its hopeful impetus ending, in Germany at least, under the boots and the bayonets of the *Freikorps* in Munich in the spring of 1919.

Needless to say, worse lay ahead: hyperinflation, the Wall Street Crash, Hitler, another World War, genocide, the atomic bombs. Much in Expressionism – not only in its catastrophic strain but also in the Messianic and Dionsyiac – looks in dread or fascination that way. The hindsight then is terrifying. And of course we are not over it yet. The diagnosis of the human condition in the early part of the twentieth century still fits pretty well at the outset of the twenty-first. And we have at our disposal now yet vaster possibilities of apocalypse.

*Poetics and Practice*

It is always the job of poetry to express what it feels like being human in a particular time and place. This requires agility; poets have to move with the times, test the old ways against the new demands, see what still works and what must be adapted and what entirely new means must be devised. In times of great acceleration, stress and dislocation, it may easily seem that nothing of the old will serve. There was a good deal in the German poetic tradition of the previous century and a half – Nature Poetry,

for example, and a tendency to raptness and elevation in tone and diction –
that could not not easily and honestly be accommodated into the new
realities. Some writers thought radical new departures would be best.
August Stramm and Kurt Schwitters, for example, by deforming and
fracturing syntax, by neologising, by condensing their lines to a single
word, tried to create an *appropriate* mode; they may be said to be aiming
at *consonance* with Modernity. Others, perhaps more interestingly,
demonstrated the incommensurability itself by employing the old forms to
treat the new moods and subjects. Their technique is more one of deliberate
discrepancy. The regular and euphonious quatrains of some of Georg Trakl
and much of Georg Heym work thus. Ernst Stadler's poem 'Small Town'
has the interface of the old and new centuries, of Nature Poetry and City
Poetry, as its very subject, in a form that seems to waver between fixed and
free. Anton Schnack's sonnets – it takes a while to recognise them as such –
are composed of very long lines monstrously overburdened with atrocious
detail; the far-apart rhymes suggest both the bravery and the near-
hopelessness of the aesthetic endeavour in that context of mechanised
modern warfare.

Two other characteristic strategies are worth mentioning.
The first – see especially Trakl and Ivan Goll – is the setting up one after
the other of more or less autonomous images; there may be no progression,
the poem consists of the sum total. This procedure is appropriately
disconcerting. It suggests a world lacking in connection; phenomena,
like the poem's images, merely coexist. And the more substantial and
autonomous these images become, the less at home in their world the human
being feels. Man exists among the phenomena, they overbear him. If he, as
poet, lends them sense or imposes sense upon them, that activity may easily

seem quite arbitrary. Significance is made up; it is not discovered, as many Romantics thought they could discover it, inherently and objectively existing in the world out there. Things have their own significance; the anthropocentric order disintegrates; the world is not there for the enlightenment or benefit of humankind.

Such strings of images individually and in total have great visual power. Adjectives are often those of vivid colour. Here the proximity to painting – several of the poets in this anthology were also painters – is very obvious. And many Expressionist poems even seem to be aspiring to the condition of painting in that they deliberately contradict the intrinsically consecutive and chronological nature of language in favour of the simultaneity or coexistence in space natural to paintings. In reading such poems – Trakl's 'Grodek', for example – the mind will be induced to hold in suspension all the images at once, as we much more easily can when looking at a picture.

Often the colours of the poems are not just bright but garish, strident – the characteristic voice of quite a lot of Expressionist poetry, particularly in its Messianic mode, is likewise vehement and hectoring. It is as though, if the poets shouted loud enough, the wished-for Saviour (the New Man, the *Übermensch*, the Ethical Socialist) would be forced to appear. Many hoped that Fraternity might be achieved not by violent revolution but by the inner transformation of every individual; and they attempted that transformation by means of loud appeal. In drama it was worse still; there, shouting and violent gestures were very normal.

Certain strains in Expressionist poetry are close to Dada and Surrealism; as in painting, violent efforts were made to express inner psychic realities, and to oppose these polemically against the dehumanising exterior world. More effective form was given to Expressionism's social engagement by the later movement or tendency known as New Sobriety. Brecht, a contradictory spirit if ever there was one, defined himself against Expressionism. First revelling nihilistically in the moral and material chaos of the post-war times, by the late 1920s he had committed himself to a creed that made sense of the world; and he devised a cooler poetics that in theatre, and better still in poetry, would serve it.

Our situation and our prospects may be no better than those the Expressionist poets of Germany faced. The onus on writers is the same: effective expression. To show; to warn; to imagine alternatives.

*David Constantine*

*Wassily Kandinsky*

### Still?

You, wild foam.
You, good-for-nothing snail, you who don't love me.
Empty silence of endless soldiers' steps, that here cannot be heard.
You, set of four windows with a cross in the middle.
You, windows of the empty hall, of the white wall where no one
leans. You, speaking windows with inaudible sighs. You ignore me:
you weren't built for me.

> You, true mortar.

You, meditative swallow, you who don't love me.
Self-consuming silence of rumbling wheels that chase and shape
the figures.
You, thousands of stones that weren't laid for me and sunk down
with hammers. You hold my feet in a spell. You are small, hard and
grey. Who gave you the power to show me the glittering gold?
You, speaking gold. You wait for me. You invite me: you were built
for me.

> You, soulful mortar.

*Trans. Elizabeth R. Napier*

**Sounds**

Face.
Far.
Cloud.
. . . .
. . . .
There stands a man with a long sword. The sword is long and also broad.
Very broad.
. . . .
. . . .
He tried to trick me many times and I admit it: He succeeded too – at tricking. And maybe too many times.
. . . .
. . . . .
Eyes, eyes, eyes … eyes.
. . . . .
. . . . .
A woman, who is thin and not young, who has a cloth on her head, which is like a shield over her face and leaves her face in shadows.
With a rope the woman leads the calf, which is still small and unsteady on its crooked legs. Sometimes the calf walks behind her very obediently. And sometimes it doesn't.
Then the woman pulls the calf by the rope. It lowers its head and shakes it and braces its legs. But its legs are weak and the rope doesn't break.
The rope doesn't break.
. . . . .
. . . . .

Eyes look out from afar.
The cloud rises.
. . . . .
. . . . . .
The face.
Afar.
The cloud.
The sword.
The rope.

*Trans. Elizabeth R. Napier*

*Wassily Kandinsky*

## Exit

You clapped your hands. Don't lean your head toward your joy.
Never, never.
And now he's cutting again with the knife.
Again he's cutting through with the knife. And now the thunder rolls in
      the sky. Who led you in deeper?
In the dark deep quiet water the tops of the trees point down.
Always. Always.
And now he sighs. A heavy sigh. Again he sighed. He sighed.
And the stick hits against something dry.
Who then will point to the door, the exit?

*Trans. Elizabeth R. Napier*

## Jacob

Jacob: a bull among his herd.
His stomping hoofs
Struck sparks of fire from the earth.

He left his speckled brothers with a roar,
Ran off across the river to the woods
Monkey bites covered him in blood.

He falls in fever, tired, riled
By the pain, his dislocated thigh:
His oxen face invents the smile.

*Trans. Rosmarie Waldrop*

### Georg Grosz

Sometimes tears of many colours
Play in his ashen eyes.

But always he encounters hearses;
They scare his dragonflies away.

He is superstitious
– Born under a great star –

His handwriting a downpour,
His drawings: letters of cloud.

As though they'd long lain in the river
His subjects bloat their bodies out.

Mysterious vagrants with tadpole mouths
And putrefied souls.

His silver fingers are
Five dreaming undertakers

But nowhere a light in the stray legend,
And yet he is a child,

The Leatherstocking Saga hero,
On intimate terms with the Redskins.

All others he hates;
They bring him bad luck.

But Georg Grosz loves his misfortune
Like a dear adversary.

And his sadness is dionysian,
Black champagne his lamentation.

He is a sea with a veiled moon.
His God seems dead, but is not so.

*Trans. Christopher Middleton*

*Else Lasker-Schüler*

## Hagar and Ishmael

Abraham's children played with shells,
Made them their mother-of-pearl canoes.
Then Isaac, suddenly afraid, hugged Ishmael,

And the two black swans sang a song
Mourning their bright world lost,
And Hagar, cast forth, had to steal her son

And shed her large tears with his small.
Their hearts gave off a sound like wells
And raced yet faster than an ostrich can.

The sun, implacable, scorched the land,
The desert's yellow hide where Hagar fell
And with white negro teeth bit the sand.

*Trans. Rosmarie Waldrop*

## Reconciliation

There will be a large star falling into my lap ...
Let us wake this night,

Pray in the languages
Which are incised like harps

Let us reconcile this night to us –
So much God overflowing ...

Our hearts are children,
They want to rest sleepysweet.

And our lips want to kiss each other
Why are you shy?

Does not my heart border on yours –
Your blood always colours my cheeks red.

Let us reconcile this night to us,
When we caress each other we don't die

There will be a large star falling into my lap.

*Trans. Esther Kinsky*

### Homesickness

I cannot speak the language
of this chilly land,
nor walk in its pace.

The clouds that drift past
I also cannot read.

Night is a stepqueen.

I always have the Pharaoh's forests on my mind
and kiss the constellations of my stars.

Already my lips are glowing
and speak distant things,

and am a colourful picture book
in your lap.

But your face weaves
a veil of weeping.

My shimmering birds'
corals have been gouged out,

on the hedgerows of the gardens
their soft nests are turning to stone.

Who will anoint my dead palaces –
they bore the crowns of my fathers,
their prayers sank into the sacred river.

*Trans. Esther Kinsky*

### To Giselheer the King

I am so alone
If I found the shadow
Of a sweet heart

– Or if someone
Gave me a star –

Always the angels
Would catch it
Back and forth.

I am afraid
Of the black earth.
How shall I go away?

Want to be buried
In the clouds,
Wherever the sun grows,

Love you so!
Do you love me?
Tell me, do – – –

*Trans. Esther Kinsky*

## The Blue Piano

I have a blue piano at home
yet I don't know a single tune.

It's been in the dark of the cellar door
since the world became so cruel.

It's played four handed by the stars
– in her boat sang the woman-moon –
in the clanging now the rats cavort.

The keyboard lies in shattered shards ...
I weep for her, dead and blue.

Dear angels, oh please open the door
– the bitter bread I chewed –
let me come to heaven alive, although
it's what you're forbidden to do.

*Trans. Esther Kinsky*

## Oh God

Everywhere only brief sleep,
In man, in greenery, in the cup of the winds.
Everyone returns home to his dead heart.

– I wish the world was still a child –
And could tell me about the first breath.

Once there was a great godliness in the sky,
The stars gave each other the bible to read.
If I could once touch the hand of God
Or see the moon on his finger.

Oh God, oh God, how far I am from you!

*Trans. Esther Kinsky*

## A Love Song

From golden breath
Heavens created us.
Oh, how we love …

Birds become buds on the branches,
And roses flutter up.

I'm always searching for your lips
Behind a thousand kisses.

A night made of gold,
Stars made of night …
No one can see us.

As the light arrives with the green
We slumber;
Only our shoulders still play like butterflies.

*Trans. Esther Kinsky*

**To the Barbarian:**

Nights when I lie
on your face,

on the steppe of your body,
plant cedars & almonds,

tireless right thru
your chest

I burrow, seek pharaoh's
gold pleasures,

your lips grown so heavy
my wonders won't ransom them,

oh take your snow skies away,
free my soul,

your diamond dreams
cut thru my veins,

I am Joseph, I wear
a sweet belt

it girdles my manycoloured
skin,

fearful roar of my shells
brings you joy

but your heart will admit
no new seas,

oh you
you!

*Trans. Pierre Joris and
Jerome Rothenberg*

**Rendez-Vous**

The doorway catches with stripe ribbons
my stick raps
tap
the straddled kerbstone
giggling
frights
through darkness
trickteasing
hastily
my thoughts
stumble
into
warm trembling.
A dark kiss
steals shyly out of the door
flicker
the street lamp
lights
after
it
up the street.

*Trans. Patrick Bridgwater*

## Love-Fight

The wanting stands
You flee and flee
Not holding
Seeking not
I
Want
You
Not!
The wanting stands
And tears the walls right down
The wanting stands
And ebbs the streams away
The wanting stands
And shrinks the miles to nil
The wanting stands
And pants and pants
And pants
Before you!
Before you
And hating
Before you
And fighting
Before you
And bowing down
And
Sinking
Treading

Stroking
Cursing
Blessing
Round about
The round round hunted world!
The wanting stands!
Process proceeds!
In selfsame cramp
Press our hands
And our tears
Well
Up
The selfsame stream!
The wanting stands!
Not you!
Not thee!
The wanting stands!
Not
I!

*Trans. Jeremy Adler*

## Primal Death

Space
Time
Space
Waying
Rising
Righting
Space
Time
Space
Stretching
Joining
Swarming
Space
Time
Space
Turning
Spurning
Racking
Space
Time
Space
Wrestling
Throwing
Throttling
Space

Time
Space
Falling
Sinking
Plunging
Space
Time
Space
Whirling
Space
Time
Space
Whirring
Space
Time
Space
Flirring
Space
Time
Space
Erring
Nil.

*Trans. Jeremy Adler*

### Dream

Through the bushes wind stars
eyes submerge film sink
whispering babbles
blossoms cleave
perfumes spray
showers deluge
winds hurry flurry scurry
sheets tear
falling startles into deep night.

*Trans. Patrick Bridgwater*

## Fickleness

My groping gropes!
Many thousand change I
I search I
and catch You
and clutch You!
Lose I.
And You and You and You
many thousand You
and always You
all ways You
mazed
maze
mazed
ever more mazed
by
this mazement
You
To You
I!

*Trans. Patrick Bridgwater*

## Desperate

Over there a glaring stone shatters
night grains glass
the times stand still
I
stone.
Far-off
you
glass!

*Trans. Patrick Bridgwater*

## Melancholy

Striding striving
living longs
shuddering standing
glances clue
dying grows
the coming
screams!
Deeply
we
dumb

*Trans. Patrick Bridgwater*

**Encounter**

Your walking smiles across to me
and
rends my heart.
Your nodding hooks and tenses.
In the shadow of your skirt
tangles
swinging
flings
flaps!
You sway and sway
my grasping snatches blindly.
The sun laughs!
And
craven wavering limps away
bereft bereft!

*Trans. Patrick Bridgwater*

### Fallen

Heaven films the eye
earth claws the hand
air hums
weeping
and
twines
women's lamentation
in
the stranded hair

*Trans. Patrick Bridgwater*

## War Instinct

Eyes flash
Your look cracks
Hot
Streams the bleeding over me
And
Drenches
Runnels of sea.
You flash and flare.
Life forces
Flame
Mildew deludes
And
Knits
And
Knits.

*Trans. Will Stone and Anthony Vivis*

## Attack

Scarves
Wave
Flutter
Chatter
Winds clatter.
Your laughter blows
Grasp hold
Scuffle force
Kiss
Surrounded
Sink down
Nothingness.

*Trans. Will Stone and Anthony Vivis*

### On Crossing the Rhine Bridge at Cologne by Night

The express train gropes and thrusts its way through darkness. Not a star is out.
The whole world's nothing but a mine-road the night has railed about
In which at times conveyors of blue light tear sudden horizons: fiery sphere
Of arc-lamps, roofs and chimneys, steaming, streaming – for seconds only clear,
And all is black again. As though we drove into Night's entrails to the seam.
Now lights reel into view … astray, disconsolate and lonely … more … and gather
… and densely gleam.
Skeletons of grey housefronts are laid bare, grow pale in the twilight, dead –
something must happen … O heavily
I feel it weigh on my brain. An oppression sings in the blood. Then all at once the
ground resounds like the sea:
All royally upborne we fly through air from darkness wrested, high up above the
river. O curve of the million lights, mute guard at the sight
Of whose flashing parade the waters go roaring down. Endless line presenting arms
by night!
Surging on like torches! Joyful! Salute of ships over the blue sea! Star-jewelled,
festive array!
Teeming, bright-eyed urged on! Till where the town with its last houses sees its
guests away.
And then the long solitudes. Bare banks. And silence. Night. Reflection. Self-
questioning. Communion. And ardour outward-flowing
To the end that blesses. To conception's rite. To pleasure's consummation. To
prayer. To the sea. To self's undoing.

*Trans. Michael Hamburger*

## Children in Front of a London Eating-House for the Poor

I saw children in a long line, ordered in pairs, standing in front of an eating-house
    for the poor,
They were waiting, silent and tired, until it was their turn for supper, and they
    could go through the door.
They were filthy and ragged and they pressed against the walls of the building.
Little girls held their thin pale babies close, in hands that were weak and fading.

They stood hungry and frightened under the lights that went on around the place.
Some had dark spots and moles that grew on a gentle face.
Their clothes smelled of scolding and starving, of light-shy rooms and of the cellar.
Their bodies were scarred by compulsory early work, and by suffering's deep
    pallor.

They waited: soon the others would be finished, and then they too would be allowed
    to go into the great hall,
Where bread and vegetables and the evening soup in tin mugs would be set in front
    of them all.
Oh, and then a big tiredness would come along and loosen their limbs' contorted
    gloom,
And the night and a good long sleep would lead them to rocking-horses, and tin
    soldiers, and a doll's house with an amazing room.

*Trans. Jeremy Adler*

## Setting Out

There was a time before, when fanfares bloodily tore apart my own impatient brain,
So that, up-rearing like a horse, it bit savagely at the rein.
Then tambourines sounded the alarm on every path
And a hail of bullets seemed the loveliest music on earth.
Then, suddenly, life stood still. Different paths were leading between the old trees.
Rooms were tempting. It was sweet to linger and sweet to rest at ease,
And, unchaining my body from reality, like some old dusty armour,
To nestle voluptuously in the down of the soft dream-hour.
But then one morning through the misty air there rolled the echo of a bugle's ring.
Hard, sharp, whistling like a sword-thrust. As if suddenly on darkness lights had
      started shining.
As if, through the tented dawn, trumpet-jolts had roused the sleeping forces,
The waking soldiers leapt up and struck their tents and busily harnessed their
      horses.
I was locked into lines like splints that thrust into morning, with fire on helmet and
      stirrup,
Forward, with battle in my blood and in my eyes, and reins held up.
Perhaps in the evening, victory marches would play around my head.
Perhaps we all would lie somewhere, stretched out among the dead.
But before the reaching out and before the sinking,
Our eyes would see their fill of world and sun, and take it in, glowing and drinking.

*Trans. Jeremy Adler*

## Small Town

The many narrow alleys that cut across
      the long through mainstreet
All run into the country.
        Everywhere the green begins.
Everywhere the sky pours in and fragrance of trees
      and the strong scent of ploughland.
Everywhere the town stops
      in a moist magnificence of pastures,

And through the grey slit between
      low roofs hills lean
With vines that climb over them and shine
      with bright supporting poles in the sunlight.
Still higher the pinewood closes in: like a thick dark
Wall to border on the red rejoicing
      of the sandstone church.

At nightfall when the factories close,
      the mainstreet is filled with people.
They walk slowly
      or in the middle of an alley they stop and stand.
They are blackened with work and engine soot.
      But their eyes uphold
Earth still, the tough power of the soil
      and the festive light of the fields.

*Trans. Christopher Middleton*

235

## Autobiography

1. Beckmann is a not very congenial character.

2. Beckmann has the misfortune to be equipped by nature with a talent not for banking, but for painting.

3. Beckmann is hard-working.

4. Beckmann has set about his training to become a European citizen in Weimar, Florence, Paris and Berlin.

5. Beckmann loves Bach, Pelikan, Piper and two or three other Germans.

6. Beckmann is a Berliner and lives in Frankfurt am Main.

7. Beckmann is married in Graz.

8. Beckmann adores Mozart.

9. Beckmann is afflicted with an inexhaustible predilection for the inadequate invention 'Life'. The new theory about the earth's atmosphere surrounded by a huge layer of nitrogen makes him heavy-hearted.

10. Beckmann has confirmed, however, that there is a 'southern light'. The idea of meteors also calms him.

11. Beckmann still sleeps very well.

*Trans. Sean Rainbird and Peter Wortsman*

## The Sun

Through the slits of my eyes a perambulator passes.
Through the slits of my eyes walks a man with a poodle.
A treeclump turns into a cluster of snakes and hisses heavenward.
A stone makes a speech. Trees in Greenbrand. Escaping islands.
A swaying and a shell-tinkling and fish-head as on the floor of the ocean.

My legs stretch out right to the horizon. A carriage bangs
away over them. My boots soar on the horizon like the towers
of a sinking town. I am the Giant Goliath. I digest goat cheese.
I am a mammoth's calf. Green grassbugs snuffle me.
Grass spans green sabers and bridges and rainbows over my belly.

My ears are giant pink shells, wide open. My body swells
with the sounds that are trapped in it. I hear the bleating
of great Pan. I hear the vermilion music of the sun. It stands
up on the left. Its wisps flash vermilion into the world's night.
When it falls it will crush the town and the church towers
and all the front gardens full of crocus and hyacinth and will blare
like the tin of children's trumpets.

But in the air there is a counter-blowing of crimson and egg-yellow
and bottle-green: swings that an orange fist holds on long threads,
and there is a singing from birdthroats that hop over branches.
A very fragile fencing of children's banners.

Tomorrow the sun will be loaded on a big-wheeled wagon
and taken to Caspari's art gallery. A beast-headed negro
with bulging neck, bladder nose and a long stride will hold fifty white
bucking asses like those yoked to wagons at the building of pyramids.

A crowd of bloodbright people will clot the streets: midwives and wetnurses,
invalids in wheelchairs, a stilting crane, two female St. Vitus dancers,
a man with a ribbed silk tie and a red-smelling policeman.

I can't stop myself: I'm full of joy. The window crossbars
shatter. A children's nurse hangs to her navel from a window.
I can't help myself: the cathedrals burst with organ fugues. I want
to make a new sun. I want to strike two together
like cymbals, and to hold my hand to my lady. Away we shall float
in a violet sedan over the roofs of your
bright yellow town in the breeze like lampshades of tissue paper.

*Trans. Christopher Middleton*

## King Solomon

with the crash of cymbals
the blare of trumpets
he broke the mute circle of demons
lit up the night
grown dim and grey with their breath

a woman we saw by his side
swaying forward receding swaying
eyes like a mummy
        ecstatic
the white peahen from Sheba

and the King himself in his tent
its entrance fringed with flames
        stretched out his arms
and the walls rose
the cedar-trunks fused

and countless beasts and devils saw
        dancing down dancing down

*Trans. Anselm Hollo*

**Waga the Serpent**

who would remember me
the Persian helmet I wore

it mirrored her image
at Paradise Gap

held back by her eyes
grey stare
            I swung the lance

hissing at me
from under the narrow shield of her pate
she came at me out of her coils

and I was suddenly gone
into her
father mother son
in one

smiling within her
dipped in the pool
by hands like those of a woman

later
            drifted out of her womb
her youngest child

*Trans. Anselm Hollo*

### Cimio

A red sky from Bucharest to Paris:
Your body is dotted with black eyes.
We hold our palms against each other like big fans whenever we make love.
Your appendix is sick, making you very yellow.

Bouquets of lilacs grow from your ears.
Your entire head is covered with lilac. You are bridled with lilac.
Your eyelids twitch and flutter like butterfly wings.
Your nose much resembles a piano key.

You have dancing hands, darling daughter.
Your narrow pelvis moves when you flutter beside me,
Gently yearning toward the wind. The great glowing women you love.
Your smile murmurs Apache songs.

In Constantsa the sea roared in your ears.
Your fingers stab like daggers, clinking glissandos in the air.
Your tongue is a red-headed snake, the burning wick of a lamp.
On your shadow, Cimio, small devils tumble
Like clicking fish emptied from a bucket onto dry land.

*Trans. Erdmute Wenzel White*

## A Bunch of Drifter Sons Hollered

A bunch of drifter sons hollered:
Always watched & fettered, the child's limbs
by a love that was but fear;
made ignorant of the use of weapons
to free ourselves
we became haters,
unredeemable.

When bloodwet we came into the world
we were more than now.
Now worries and prayers
have circumcised & diminished us.

We live small.
We want small.
And our feeling like tame cattle eats
in will's hand.

But at times desires
grown strong in our earliest blood
spread eagle-like their wings
as if wanting to dare a flight
beyond earth's shadow.
Yet earth, the mother of worries and prayers,
your ally,
does not release them from her wrinkled old body.
But I desire my own blood.
I do not allow other gods besides me.

Meaning: to be a son: to be scoffed at by one's blood:
Cowardly lord, cowardly lord!
Crimson-veiled my beauty stands
day and night for you.
Why do you tremble?
I trained myself nimble sinews
for your wishes,
o, let me have them!
Let me dance!
Sweep my room.
Yellow drooling skeletons
of whitehaired, gloomyglum blood
threaten me.
But I want to dance
through you,
veilless
your blood.

*Trans. Pierre Joris*

**Happy Youth**

The mouth of a girl who had lain a long time in
        the rushes
looked so nibbled away.
The breasts broken open, the feed-pipe so full of
        holes.
Finally in a copse under the diaphragm
was discovered a nest of young rats.
One sister ratlet lay dead.
The others lived off liver and kidneys,
drank the cold blood and had
spent a happy youth here.
And short and sweet their death was too:
The whole pack were thrown into the water.
Oh! how the little snouts squeaked!

*Trans. R. J. Kavanagh*

### Little Aster

A drowned drayman was humped on to the slab.
Someone or other had jammed a dark light violet aster
between his teeth.
And as I, working
with a long knife
under the skin from the breast,
cut out tongue and gums,
I must have knocked it for it slid
into the adjacent brain.
I tucked it into his breast cavity for him
between the cotton wads
as he was being sewn up again.
Drink your fill in your vase!
Rest in peace,
Little aster!

*Trans. R. J. Kavanagh*

## Underground Train

The softening shudders. Early flowers. As
from warm pelts it issues from the forests.
A red swarms up. The great blood rises.

Through all this spring there comes a strange woman.
The stockinged instep's there. But where it ends
is far from me. I sob at the entrance.
Half-hearted flowering, strange dampnesses.

Oh how her mouth squanders the luke-warm air!
You rose-brain, sea-blood, you twilight goddess.
You bed of earth, how coolly your hips stream
forth the passage in which you walk.

Dark: now there is life under her clothes:
All white animal, let loose and voiceless scent.

A wretched dog-brain, heavy hung with god.
My forehead wearies me. Oh that gently she'd
let loose a battery of blossom thrusts
to join the swelling and shudder and ooze.

Left so loose. So tired. I long to wander.
Bloodless the paths. Melodies from stray gardens.
Shadows and the Flood. Distant joys, a dying
away in the ocean's freeing deep azure.

*Trans. R. J. Kavanagh*

## Palau

'Evening is red on the island of Palau
and the shadows sink –'
sing, from woman's chalices too
it is good to drink,
deathly the little owls cry
and the death-watch ticks out,
very soon it will be
Lemurs and night.

Hot these reefs. From eucalypti there flows
a tropical palm concoction,
all that still holds and stays
also longs for destruction
down to the limbless stage,
down to the vacuum,
back to the primal age,
dark ocean's womb.

Evening is red on the island of Palau,
in the gleam of these shadows
there issues rising from twilight and dew:
'Never and Always,'
all the deaths of the earth
are fords and ferries,
what to you owes its birth
surrounded with strangeness –

Once with sacrificial
fat on the pinewood floor
your bed of flames would travel
like wine to the shore,
megaliths heaped around
and the graves and the halls,
hammer of Thor that's bound
for the Aesir, crumbled, falls –

As the gods surcease,
the great Caesars decline,
from the cheek of Zeus
once raised up to reign –
sing, already the world
to the strangest rhythm is swung,
Charon's coin if not curled
long tasted under the tongue.

Coupling. Sepias your seas
and coral animate,
all that still holds and sways
also longs to disintegrate,
evening is red on the island of Palau,
eucalyptus glaze
raises in runes from twilight and dew:
Never and Always.

*Trans. Michael Hamburger*

*Oskar Kokoschka*

**From** **The Dreaming Boys**
*Dedicated to Gustav Klimt as a token of admiration*

little red fish
little fish red
with my triple-edged knife i stab you dead
with my fingers asunder rend
to bring your mute circling to an end

little red fish
little fish red
my little knife is red
my little fingers are red
in the bowl a little fish sinks down dead

and i fell down and dreamed
destiny has many pockets
i am waiting beside a peruvian stone tree
its many-fingered leaf-arms stretch out like fearful arms and
    fingers of thin
yellow figures
stirring imperceptibly in the star-flowered bushes
    as blind men stir
without a bright
departing streak in the dark air of falling
    starflowers luring the mute animals
blood-frenzied she-beasts
slipping away
in fours and fives out of green
breathing sea-forest
with its silent rain

above the forest waves pursue their crashing course
                through the rootless
red-flowered
countless air-branches
which like hair dip sucking into the seawater
where green rollers writhe their way out
and the terrible ocean of depths and
                man-eating fish
seizes the overcrowded galley
                up on the masts swing cages with little
                blue birds
pulls on the iron chains and dances with it
                out into the typhoons, where
                water columns like ghost snakes walk on the
                roaring waters
i hear the calls of the sailors
heading for the lands where birds can talk
the sails tossed this way and tossed that
cold air stirred them and twisted the canvas
the ship docks
softly and in step
at intervals audible
then at times drowned out go the processions of those
                disembarking
fawners in brown woollen clothes worm their way through
                and naked skinny girls give birds
nuts and coral necklaces in memory

of the nights of dark caresses
and i fell and dreamed the sick night

why do you sleep
blue-clad men
under the branches of dark walnut trees in the moonlight?

you gentle women
what is that welling up in your red coats
in your bodies the expectation of entwined limbs
since yesterday and time immemorial?
do you feel the excited heat of the quivering
mild air
– i am the circling werewolf –

when the sound of the evening bell fades
i creep into your gardens
into your pastures
i break into your peaceable kraal

my body divested of its harness
my body enhanced with blood and paint
crawls into your bowers
swarms through your villages
crawls into your souls
swarms in your bodies

*Trans. Michael Mitchell*

**Summer**

Evenings the cuckoo's complaint
Fades from the woods.
Wheat bends lower.
The red poppies.

Black clouds threaten
Above the hill.
The old song of the cricket
Dies away in the fields.

The chestnut leaves
Never stir.
On the winding stair
Your dress rustles.

Candle burning quietly
In the dark room –
A silver hand
Snuffs it out.

Windless unstarry night.

*Trans. Keith Waldrop*

## To the Silenced

O the insanity of the great city, where at nightfall
Against black walls the stunted trees stiffen,
The spirit of evil peers from a silver mask;
Light with magnetic scourge drives out
The stony night.
O the sunken tolling of evening bells.

Whore, who bears a dead child
In icy convulsions.
God's wrath with screaming whips
Over the brows of those possessed.
Purple plague, hunger, that ruptures green eyes,
O the gruesome laughter of gold.

But in dark caves a mankind more silent bleeds,
From hard metals forms the redeeming head.

*Trans. Will Stone*

# Night

I sing you wild fissure,
In the night storm
Soaring mountains;
You grey towers
Spilling with hellish grimaces,
Animals aflame,
Harsh ferns, spruces,
Crystal flowers.
Agony everlasting,
That you hunt for God,
Tender spirit,
Sighing in the falls,
Among the surging pines.
Golden flares the fire
About the gathered peoples.
Above blackish outcrops
Drunk with death
Plunges the glowing-wind bride,
The blue surge
Of the glacier
And powerfully sounds the bell
In the valleys:
Flames, curses
And the dark play of lust,
A hardened head
Storms heaven.

*Trans. Will Stone*

*Georg Trakl*

### To the Boy Elis

Elis, when the blackbird calls in the black wood,
This is your downfall.
Your lips drink in the coolness of the blue rockspring.

Leave be, when quietly your brow bleeds
Bygone legends
And the dark interpretation of bird flight.

But you walk with soft steps into the night,
Which is heavy with purple grapes,
And move your arms more beautifully in the blue.

A thornbush sounds,
Where your moon eyes are.
O, how long, Elis, have you been dead.

Your body is a hyacinth,
Into which a monk dips his waxen fingers.
A black cavern is our silence,

From which at times a gentle animal steps
And slowly lowers heavy lids.
On your temples black dew drips,

The final gold of failed stars.

*Trans. Will Stone*

**Eastern Front**

The wrath of the people is dark,
Like the wild organ notes of winter storm,
The battle's crimson wave, a naked
Forest of stars.

With ravaged brows, with silver arms
To dying soldiers night comes beckoning.
In the shade of the autumn ash
Ghosts of the fallen are sighing.

Thorny wilderness girdles the town about.
From bloody doorsteps the moon
Chases terrified women.
Wild wolves have poured through the gates.

*Trans. Christopher Middleton*

### De Profundis

There is a stubblefield where a black rain falls.
There is a brown tree here, which stands alone.
There is a hissing wind that wreathes the empty huts –
How sorrowful this evening.

Beyond the hamlet
The gentle orphan still gathers in the meagre grain.
Round and golden her eyes graze in the twilight
And her womb awaits the heavenly bridegroom.

Returning home
Shepherds found the sweet remains
Decayed in the thornbush.

A shadow I am far from darkened villages.
God's silence
I drank from the spring in the grove.

Onto my brow cold metal steps.
Spiders seek my heart.
There is a light that dies in my mouth.

At night I found myself upon a heath,
Thick with filth and stardust.
In the hazel copse
Crystal angels have chimed again.

*Trans. Will Stone*

### Decline

*To Karl Borromäus Heinrich*

Over the white pond
The wild birds have travelled on.
In the evening an icy wind blows from our stars.

Over our graves
The broken brow of the night inclines.
Under oak trees we sway in a silver boat.

Always the town's white walls resound.
Under arches of thorns,
O my brother, blind minute-hands,
We climb towards midnight.

*Trans. Michael Hamburger*

## Complaint

Sleep and death, doleful eagles
Wing nightlong around this head:
Eternity, an icy wave,
Would engulf the golden
Image of mankind. Livid flesh
Is battered on dreadful shoals.
And the dark voice lifts a complaint
Over the waters.
Sister of stormy melancholy, see
How a fearful craft is scuttled
Underneath the stars,
The night's quiet countenance.

*Trans. Keith Waldrop*

## Occident

*For Else Lasker-Schüler*

I

Moon, as if a dead thing
Stepped out of a blue cave,
And many blossoms fall
Across the rocky path.
Silver a sick thing weeps
By the evening pond,
In a black boat
Lovers crossed over to death.

Or the footsteps of Elis
Ring through the grove
The hyacinthine
To fade again under oaks.
O the shape of that boy
Formed out of crystal tears,
Nocturnal shadows.
Jagged lightning illumines his temples
The ever-cool,
When on verdant hill
Springtime thunder resounds.

II

So quiet are the green woods
Of our homeland,
The crystal wave
That dies against a perished wall
And we have wept in our sleep;

Wander with hesitant steps
Along the thorny hedge
Singers in the evening summer
In holy peace
Of the vineyards distantly gleaming;
Shadows now in the cool lap
Of night, eagles that mourn.
So quietly does a moonbeam close
The purple wounds of sadness.

III
You mighty cities
Stone on stone raised up
In the plain!
So quietly
With darkened forehead
The outcast follows the wind,
Bare trees on the hillside.
You rivers distantly fading!
Gruesome sunset red
Is breeding fear
In the thunderclouds.
You dying peoples!
Pallid billow
That breaks on the beaches of Night,
Stars that are falling.

*Trans. Michael Hamburger*

**Grodek**

At nightfall the autumn woods cry out
With deadly weapons and the golden plains,
The deep blue lakes, above which more darkly
Rolls the sun; the night embraces
Dying warriors, the wild lament
Of their broken mouths.
But quietly there in the pastureland
Red clouds in which an angry god resides,
The shed blood gathers, lunar coolness.
All the roads lead to blackest carrion.
Under golden twigs of the night and stars
The sister's shade now sways through the silent copse
To greet the ghosts of the heroes, the bleeding heads;
And softly the dark flutes of autumn sound in the reeds.
O prouder grief! You brazen altars,
Today a great pain feeds the hot flame of the spirit,
The grandsons yet unborn.

*Trans. Michael Hamburger*

*Jakob van Hoddis*

### End of the World

From pointed pates hats fly into the blue,
All winds resound as though with muffled cries.
Steeplejacks fall from roofs and break in two,
And on the coasts – we read – flood waters rise.

The storm has come, the seas run wild and skip
Landwards, to squash big jetties there.
Most people have a cold, their noses drip.
Trains tumble from the bridges everywhere.

*Trans. Michael Hamburger*

## Last Watch

How dark are your temples,
and how heavy your hands.
Far now you have travelled
where my words do not sound.

Under the flame that wavers
so sad and old you lie,
your lips shrunken forever
in bitter fixity.

Tomorrow will come a silence
and the air hold a faint
rustle perhaps of garlands
and a decaying scent.

But hollower now year by year
will nights be left
here where your head lay and always
you breathed so soft.

*Trans. Anthony Hasler*

## The Prisoners I

They tramp the courtyard's narrow circling track.
Their vision flickers in the barren space.
It searches for some tree, grassy place,
and then the wall's bald whiteness beats it back.

Their footprints trace a black unending arc
like a wheel's endless turning in a mill.
And like a monk's shaven and tonsured skull
the middle of the yard sits bald and stark.

Thin rain spatters their meagre uniforms.
Their sombre gaze ascends the high grey wall
where boxes front the windows, dark and small
like a vast beehive's blackened honeycombs.

They drive them in, like sheep before the shears.
Grey shoulders press and thrust into the shed.
And echoes ring and rattle with the tread
of wooden clogs upon the landing-floors.

*Trans. Anthony Hasler*

## Berlin I

The road's high verge, there where we lay,
was white with dust. We looked into the crush
of countless bodies, saw them course and rush,
the metropolis tower far in the sinking day.

Through the chaos crowded coaches pushed,
Festooned with paper flags in bright display.
Omnibuses, body and roof piled high.
Automobiles, fumes, horns bright and harsh.

To the giant sea of stone. But to the west
We saw in the treeline on the road's long rim,
The filigree of boughs whose leaves were lost.

The ball of the sun hung vast at heaven's seam.
Out of the sunset's road red streamers burst.
On all the heads there lay the light's last dream.

*Trans. Anthony Hasler*

### The Demons of the Cities

They wander through the cities and the night.
The cities cower from their plunging foot.
About their chins the blackened cloud-racks meet
like sailors' beards besmeared with smoke and soot.

Upon the rooftop sea their shadow sways.
Along the street it crawls like mist to douse
the rows of lamps, burdens the cobbled ways,
groping a slow path forward house by house.

With one foot stamping heavy on a square,
one crooked knee resting high upon a tower,
they fill the sky, blowing pan-pipes that blare
into the storm-clouds and the rain's black shower.

Circling their feet a ritornello sounds,
drab music from the city's sea beneath.
It rises in the dark, its shifting tones
now dulled, now shrill, a mighty song of death.

They walk beside the river, black and wide,
a torpid, heaving reptile, its long back
glinting with yellow lamplight as it slides
through night that veils the sky in mourning black.

They rest their bulk against a parapet
upon a bridge, and thrust into the mass
of men their hands, like fauns, who by some wet
swamp plunge a questing arm in the morass.

One stands. Before the white moon he suspends
a black mask. And the houses all retreat
into a deep, dim shaft, as night descends
to crush them from the sky, a leaden sheet.

The cities' shoulders snap. A roof-peak cracks.
The broken housetop washes red with flame.
They straddle it, and hurl like midnight cats
towards the firmament their frenzied scream.

Up in a room crowded with dark and shadows
a woman moans in pain. Her time is near.
Her body towers giant from the pillows,
while the great devils stand and circle her.

Shuddering she clings close to her torment's bed,
and screams. The room is shaking with her fits.
The foetus comes. Her womb yawns long and red.
About its fruit her bleeding body splits.

The devils stretch necks forward like giraffes.
The newborn has no head. She gazes down,
then tumbles back numb as a terror grasps
frog-fingered at the column of her spine.

But the great demons swell to monstrous height.
Their horns tear red the sky and break the stars.
Their pounding hooves strike fire. Earthquakes fight
and through the womb of cities thunder roars.

*Trans. Anthony Hasler*

## Blue. White. Green.

In a green meadow a little wood
Where white birches reach for sunlight:
Early green, pale on slender branches –
Like a cloud, like the finest fleece.

White clouds grow into the air
Like mountains rising baseless from blue lakes.
Banks, wooded, dissolve in light,
Their dusky shadows sunk in fragrant blue.

*Trans. Keith Waldrop*

## Robespierre

He bleats under his breath. Eyes fixed on the
Straw in the cart. His teeth grind white slime.
Gulps till his cheeks are hollowed.
One foot hangs naked through the slats.

Every jolt of the cart sends him flying.
The chains on his arms rattle then like bells.
Children yelp with laughter – their mothers
Hold them up to see over the crowd.

Someone tickles his foot. He doesn't notice.
Now the cart stops. His eyes lift and he sees
At the end of the street the black machine.

His forehead, ashen, beads with sweat.
His mouth goes weird in his dreadful face.
They wait for screams. They hear no sound.

*Trans. Keith Waldrop*

**Hunger**

Has caught a dog, wrenches
Red jaws. Blue tongue thrust
Out. Rolls in dirt. Sucks
Withered grass ripped out of sand.

Empty gullet seeping
Drop after drop of fire
To his guts. Then a fist
Twists his hot neck into ice.

Stumbles through steam. Sun a blur, red
Oven door. Green half-moon
Dances at his eyes. Done for.

Black hole, cold, staring.
Falls, even fallen feels
Panic squeeze tighter.

*Trans. Keith Waldrop*

**Wound Roses Roses Bleed**
**Poem 23**

> Wound roses roses bleed
> Wound colossus wound wound
> Roses languish languish roses
> Torrid wound torrid torrid
> Languish roses languish languish
> Wound torrid wound wound
> Roses torrid torrid roses
> Embers trickle trickle ember
> Embers trickle trickle ember
> Bleed roses wound torrid
> Languish wounds rose blood
> Night languish roses night
> Night wound blood blood
> Night bleed night
> Blood night blood
> Blood bleeds
> Blood
>
> Silversound
> Wildwoodwondrous silversound
> Wildwoodsoothing silversound
>
> Silence trickle blood

*Trans. Jerome Rothenberg*

**Evening**
**Poem 25**

Glow caresses soft worlds kiss
Whistle Sun Thread Sun (Zeppelin)
I Thread Sun glimmerglare
And glimmerglows softens world.

*Trans. Pierre Joris*

**Repose**

A little white cloud drops down from me.
In the valley I lie under lilies and call.
The breath from her hand shakes in the wind.
A big black cloud drops into the pot.
That the hangman's apprentice may bake it,
that it may be changed to ashes
and die.

*Trans. Jerome Rothenberg*

**For Franz Marc**

cat

        legs

catlegs humans joy

humans world the earth round out the cats

cats paw the grovelld grass

cross thready string

brains joys meows of twentythousand cats

ink paws turn tail spaces cats

and spaces, spaces, spaces cats

and cats, cats, cats spaces

and paws, paws, paws lights

and human

*Trans. Jerome Rothenberg*

### The Bird Plus Three

woe our good kaspar is dead.

who's going to bear the burning banner in his pigtail. who's going to turn the coffee-mill. who's going to entice the idyllic deer.

on the sea he confused the ships with the little word parapluie and he called the winds bee-father.

woe woe woe our good kaspar is dead. holy bim-bam kaspar is dead.

the hayfish clatter in the bells when his fore-name is uttered so i keep on sighing kaspar kaspar kaspar.

why have you turned into a star or a water-chain or an udder of black light or a transparent slate on the groaning drum of rocky being.

now our heads and our toes are shrivelling up and the fays lie half charred on the funeral pyres. now the black bowling alley is thundered behind the sun and there is no one left to wind up the compasses and cartwheels.

who's going to eat with the rat now at the solitary table. who's going to chase away the devil when he tries to lead the horses astray. who's going to explain to us the monograms in the stars.

his bust will grace the fireplaces of all truly noble men but that is small consolation and snuff for a death's head.

*Trans. R.W. Last*

### I am a Horse

i am riding in a train
and it is packed.
in my compartment
every seat is taken by a lady
on whose lap a gentleman sits.
the air is unbearably tropical.
all the passengers
are terribly hungry
and eat incessantly.
suddenly the gentlemen start
to mope and whine
and demand the maternal breast.
they unbutton the ladies' dresses
and suckle fresh milk to their hearts' delight.
but i am not suckling
and i am not being suckled.
no one is sitting on my lap
and i am not sitting on anyone's lap
for i am a horse.
i am sitting big and upright

my back legs on the railway seat
and my forelegs
comfortably propping me up.
i whinny out loud hee haw.
on my breast glitter
the sex-buttons of sex-appeal
in pretty rows
like glittering buttons of a uniform.
o summertime.
o big wide world.

*Trans. R.W. Last*

**(Untitled)**

the nightbirds carry burning lanterns in the cross-beams of their eyes.
they drive delicate ghosts and travel on tender-veined coaches.
the black coach is harnessed before the mountain.
the black bell is harnessed before the mountain.
the black rocking-horse is harnessed before the mountain.
the dead carry saws and tree-trunks across to the jetty.
out of the crops of the birds the harvests tumble on to the iron threshing-floors.
the angels land in baskets of air.
the fish put on their walking-shoes and roll in stars towards the exit.

*Trans. R.W. Last*

**Self Portrait 1**

I am everything at once, but never will I do everything at once.

**Self Portrait 2**

An interminable dreaming of life's sweetest excess –
restless – with anxious inward pain, in the soul. – blazes,
burns, alert after battle, – heart spasm. Weigh it all up –
and madly active with activated lust, – powerless is the
torment of thought, meaningless to extend thought. –
Speak the language of the creator and give. – Daemons!
Break their power! –
Your language. – Your signs. – Your might.

*Trans. Will Stone and Anthony Vivis*

## Visions

Everything was dear to me –
I wanted to look at the angry lovingly,
so that their eyes must reciprocate;
and I wanted to offer gifts to the envious and tell them
I am worthless.

… I heard tender swelling winds sweep through
lines of air.
And the girl
who read aloud in a lamenting voice
and the infants,
who gazed at me with huge eyes and on my return look
snuggled up,
and the far off clouds,
which gazed upon me with virtuous folded eyes.

The white pallid girls showed me their black
legs and red garters
and spoke with black fingers.
I, however pondered the far worlds
of finger flowers –
and whether I myself am there
I was hardly aware.

I saw the park: yellow-green, blue-green, red-green, violet-green,
sunny-green and shudder-green –
and listened to the blossoming orange flowers,
then I bound myself to the oval park wall and listened
to the gaunt-footed children,
who were touched with blue and streaked with grey
by the pink bows.
The tree column led lines exactly where they sat down
long around.
I pondered my coloured portrait visions,
and it struck me
that only once had I spoken
to all of them.

*Trans. Will Stone and Anthony Vivis*

## Music while Drowning

In no time the black river yoked all my strength
I saw the lesser waters great and the soft banks steep and high.

Twisting I fought
and heard the waters within me,
the fine, beautiful black waters –
then I breathed golden strength once more.
The river ran rigid and more strongly.

*Trans. Will Stone and Anthony Vivis*

## Bloodhound

Bloodhound in front of my heart
Watching over my fire
You that feed on bitter kidneys
In the suburb of my misery

With the wet flame of your tongue lick
The salt of my sweat
The sugar of my death

Bloodhound in my flesh
Catch the dreams that fly off from me
Bark at the white ghosts
Bring back to their pen
All my gazelles

And savage the ankles of my fleeting angel

*Trans. Michael Hamburger*

## The Cinema Manager
*Dithyramb*

Paradise is yours for a dime. This is the world's one and only paradise: Chemnitzer Street No. 136. The golden letters shine out loud.

To the box office! The lady's got real diamond rings. She gives everyone her crimson smile, you, sweat-stained porter, as well as you, wooden soldier. She wants to be everyone's blonde sweetheart: for a dime.

The world is yours. The doorman in red dress-coat is your slave. You'll feel just like the Emperor when he steps inside his castle.

Only here are happy people. For a dime, oh brothers, you, too, can see happy people.

There ladies gently fan themselves across sunny parks. Streets, heavenly spirals, raise passers-by above the earth. Even a dog will be your loyal brother: a dog!

You, the downcast, the same fate suddenly binds you all to God. For a dime you all can buy profoundest fate!

And see: you shall be angelic. Here in the cinema you are beyond earth. Good and evil in life are nothing but a reflex like black and white on this screen. Nothing is. Everything is!

Sure, everyone's got a dime. Even the lemonade seller has a dime left over. And the maid can pay with her tip.

I give you God's creation: paradise without snake and apple. Curse this smiling sceptic who taps the screen and says: that's a white sheet! Curse this liar: because that's life, no life is more real.

That's life: with jungles galore and where Niagara Falls roar. Where on the hot race track a jockey breaks his neck. Where a murderer in tails begins to weep.

That's life: with infinite pity you sit by starving widows. With infinite pity you bend over the banker who was forced to steal, poor man!

That is God's creation. Oh orchestra of paradise! The violins sob love. Flutes pitch like dragonflies across the cello's pond.

And I: see in me the apostle. See how I fight and suffer and die because of you. I have to give you all my soul for a dime.

I have to roll out the cosmos for you.

I have to rouse all your pleasures. I am God's prompter.

If I had a dime how cheerful I would be. All it costs is a dime. Cassandra sits in the box-office and will smile at you. Give her a dime.

*Trans. Martin Chalmers*

**Poem in Prose**

Yellow schnapps still smoulders in your mouths. Whore's
blood still hungers in your eyes. Behind you are torment and
pain and need.

Behind you lies smashed the house of nights. The asphalt hells
have tumbled down. All winters turned to slippery thaw.

You liquor stench alleys are purged. The mystic factories shiver
naked. The chimneys' stony arms trail slackly.

Past spring seasons on railway embankment slopes. You, the
starving, in front of full bakeries! Oh you poor sleepers of
Sunday mornings!

Arise! The sun piles up burning pyres for you. The pavement
serenades you under your dancing boots. Oh all of you!

Hot youths talk easily in the crowd. Men wear sun turbans
round their short hair. Oh the time is new. And man is great.

The tyrant hangs on red factory chimneys. Sweating brokers
must polish the heavy ingots of gold. And the proletarians
go before.

The early morning rays play green around your temples. Work
glows in accord with your strong muscles. And mankind's love
is ready.

*Trans. Martin Chalmers*

## Journey into Misery

Yet how the solitude of man torments
When landscapes with a sorrow like your own turn from you
And shrink into themselves, are so estranged!
A station, small, may push you out into cold rain,
A goods truck, empty and futureless, may ask for alms.
There on the dark ploughland crawls a sallow nag,
O if only he knew that you exist
And love him, he would sprout blue wings to heaven.
Sometimes with large eyes water may look up at you,
And since it did not see your smile,
Into itself it falls back flat and joyless.
So you leave each thing there alone. Fate hurries you on.
The old hunchback on the road, forever she'll watch you go,
On the slant gable the loud placard stands inconsolable.
So you leave all things there alone in loving and unanswered
                humbleness
Solitary yourself, for whom a town is waiting
Where in your cheap hotel you'll sob the long night through.

*Trans. Christopher Middleton*

## Ode to Berlin

Your asphalt heart
Proles hurl it through the glass panes of the century
And your electric eye shines above hanging gardens
Yellow underground train
Flees to sweet sources of the evening

Berlin you bar of the planet
How I scent the primeval!
The omnibus rises from underworlds
Brains baked brown at Kempinsky

Fat fingered prophet
Over Prussian blue post office clerk
Brother: oh heaven's axis is wavering
Snap your top hat shut

But in the cinema kings are being crowned still
Kant and Einstein smile popularly
Culture! Culture! Culture!
Wire your lies to the negroes

Little girls have a paper heart
Shaded paradise of promenade benches
The brothel keeper
Loves your spring seasons of tulle and linden blossoms!

The colossal must be bursting with marble!
There are neither towers nor gods:
But the quadrangle of the bank, gaol of Moabit:
And the statue of the policeman
Beside the Stollwerck chocolate slot machines
Looks Egyptian

Then my prole wells up out of the schnapps den
Freedom! chews the tired muzzle of hunger
Freedom! chirps the distant artillery
Freedom! in columns advancing at the double

The red editor pens hymns!
And the organs thunder: O Susannah!
Holy roses bloom in the Landwehr Canal
Last rose of Germany!

Everything gold dissolved into free beer
Loosening the asphalt of the mob –
Oh Berlin, you nettle at the crossroads of the east
Wither from your dust crumble forgetfulness

*Trans. Martin Chalmers*

DIE LEBENDEN DEM TOTEN . ERINNERUNG AN DEN 15. JANUAR 1919

## Underworld

The golden car glides like a barge on a deep nocturnal boulevard.
Mountains thunder in the night, lashed by our sharp light.
Into ravines we plunge with outspread angels' wings.
There is the cabaret. And godlike are we clothed in a cloud.
Oh already at the door stands the tailcoat with his thousand humps.
From a reciter's black mouth issues the stale rot-gut reek of the outskirts.
The wedding and the funeral of tear-stained seamstresses.
Then cupid flings wide golden doors, and pink dancers kick out legs like
      seraphim.
You at the bar, once a cocotte, pale in the basket of frozen anemones,
Staring with huge round eyes like a night insect among the roses,
You be the torch of our dance of death.
Yet deeper still whirl the shadows, ever darker.
A worker taps me on the shoulder: 'Ho, comrade, salut!'
A mason, he had just come up out of the subway tunnel in a white,
      white glistening apron.
Yet a black spot burns hot on it, his starved heart.
Music! Music! The earth is petrified music!
I shall set it free again with the beautiful names of whores.
Oh tailcoat, why do you smile? My life's gold melted in your hell.
Oh car, impatient barge, which bears us down to the black earth again!

*Trans. Martin Chalmers*

## Nightscape

A constellation like a day; and behind it a horizon by light and
      flare fingered and shrouded,
Which went or came, fell or stood, restless, spectral; and if it
      went, there was deep night;
And if it came, a forest was made, somewhere a village lay
      looking furtive and white,
And a valley full of sleep, with torrents, tangled things, with
      graves and towers of churches, in ruins, with rising
      mists, moist and big-clouded,
With huts where sleeping men lay, where a dream walked, full of
      fever, full of strangeness, full of animal splendour,
      where there suddenly burst
Open a curtain of clouds; behind it rose a sea of stars or a realm
      of rockets, a light sprang up out of the ravine,
Terrible, roaring, wheel-clatter rattled on roads, a man stepped
      darkly into the dark, his face dazed with the dread of
      what he had seen,
Saw the flight of questing fires, heard butchery down below, saw
      behind the darkness the city by fire forever accurst.
Heard a rumbling in the belly of the earth, ponderous, powerful,
      primal, heard traffic on roads, heading into the void,
      into the extended night, into a storm, dreadful in the
      West. – Unquiet the ear
With the thousand hammers of the front, with the riders who
      came, stamping, head-long, with the riders who rode
      away to turn into shadows, engulfed by the night,
      to decompose,

Death slaughters them, leaving them lying among weeds,
weighty, fossilised, hands full of spiders, mouths
crusted brown,
Eyes full of bottomless sleep, on their brows the bloom of
obfuscation, blue, waxen, decaying in the smoke
of night,
Which sank down, which shed its shadows far, which stretched
vaulting from hill to hill, over woods and decay, over
brains full of dreams, over the hundred dead,
without repose,
Over the uncounted fires, over laughter and madness, over
crosses in fields, over pain and despair, over rubble
and ash, over river and ruined town …

*Trans. Patrick Bridgwater*

## Screams

There were nights quite shattered with screams, with great screams of death,
    coming brokenly from the bottom of men's hearts, demented and full of
    grief,
Dark human sounds in which affliction sang, red and northern, screams in which
    oceans raged and sheets of fire.
Were they calling their gay childhood? Secret paths in the woods? Screams which
    came night after night, eerie, growing ever weaker, ever fainter, coming from
    far beyond the wire
In front of which death grew, slowly, overwhelmingly and pitilessly, death by
    bleeding, death by starvation, death by loneliness, suffering beyond belief –
Who crawled out towards the mouth that screamed? No one, because the rifles
    rattled incessantly on this side and the other, because death rode incessantly
    through night and hours with flares festooned.
Who broke out in tears at that terrible 'Help', 'Have pity', 'Save me', 'Mercy'?
    Striking the heart like the song of dying birds, southern, lost, and alone in
    their plight –
Death covered them with corrosion, green mud-death; in their screams pennons
    fluttered, sandhills lay, children's balls bounced, and girlfriends' blouses
    gleamed white …
Every nightfall still this is in my ears; why did I not die of it? Of this: exhausted
    nights, torturing cries, smoke over helmets, stars, acrid, over fatal neck-
    wound,
Air filled with moaning as they hung torn to shreds in the wire, flapping in the wind,
    with thighs laid open … Who thought up all this? These nights full of danger,
These nights full of cruelty, shameful madness? Rotted like weeds beneath night's
    vaults of red and yellow light,

To whom were their curses addressed? To whom were their prayers addressed? To
a god who did not hear, who lay asleep on cloudhills. To whom were their
screams directed? To heartless men who went on firing, round after round,
Into the great darkness ... O, that heaven did not burst open, that the earth did not
open up on to which their screaming oozed, far-off and ever stranger,
O that their mothers did not come, faces lined with grief, that their children did not
cry their hearts out. Nothing could dislodge the blight
Which bade them scream, long drawn-out, dreadful, ending in a choking rattle.
Stars hung silver among them, a white play of lights. If a brow hung out, it
was soon shrouded in smoke and sound ...

*Trans. Patrick Bridgwater*

# Afterword

They did not look.
They envisioned.
They did not photograph.
They had visions.
Instead of the rocket they created the perpetual state of excitement.
*Kasimir Edschmid*[1]

Our main objective in compiling *Music while drowning* has been to gather together a representative selection of German poetry from the Expressionist years in English translation, within a relatively brief space.[2] We are using German as a linguistic, rather than geographic, term (including Austrian poets, an Alsatian poet and a Russian poet writing in German). We have chosen to concentrate on poets writing in the approximate time span 1910 to 1930 (with some work from either side of this period), and from throughout the German-speaking world.[3] We have placed particular emphasis on a number of poets – Georg Heym, Ernst Stadler, August Stramm, Georg Trakl, Else Lasker-Schüler, Gottfried Benn, Ivan Goll – while leaving room for interestingly relevant works by other poets. The 'visions' and 'the perpetual state of excitement' referred to by Kasimir Edschmid are realised in their works in an especially powerful way, however dark and tragic the form those visions may take – and their poetry has been available to us in a sufficient quantity of excellent translations.

We have interpreted 'Expressionism' loosely rather than strictly, with a view to being inclusive. This is especially the case with regard to poets whose work emerged from Expressionism or is otherwise related to it, while often moving away from it in some respects. We are thinking here of Hugo Ball, Kurt Schwitters and Hans Arp – poets more usually associated with Dadaism.[4] At the same time, we chose – or else found ourselves forced – to omit certain poets variously associated with Expressionism, such as Theodor Däubler, Alfred Mombert, Alfred Lichtenstein, Franz Werfel and Johannes R. Becher. There are a number of reasons, ranging from availability of suitable translations to problems of space; however, we also exercised our own artistic or poetic preferences. We omitted Rainer Maria Rilke, some of whose work may relate to Expressionism but is very widely available elsewhere in translation. Other important German language poets of the period, such as Bertolt Brecht and Stefan George, were not included, either because their work is similarly available through other sources or because their poetry does not relate to Expressionism in significant ways.

Our sense of the way that the limits and counter-limits of Expressionism might be drawn intersects with an awareness that 'Expressionist' is, in fact, a much used but ultimately rather vague term. However, it is also a term that aptly refers us to the range of emotions and artistic responses to the atmosphere of trauma and distress both before 1914 and after 1918 in Germany, as well as to the outbreak and terrible experience of war itself.[5] Equally, it refers us to a grouping of poets and artists, which was based on friendships, loves, shared concerns, café culture and specific journals. For example, both the Café de Westens in Berlin and the journal *Die Aktion* were crucial for the explosion of Expressionist activity: the former a place where many of the writers and artists met, the latter a platform for their work. Expressionism overlapped with 'The Blue Rider' group, shared some concerns with Dada, and was one of the roots of the early Bauhaus – the term is thus both precise *and* vague. There was undoubtedly an upsurge of literary and artistic activity from about 1905 that peaked in the decade around the First World War and the subsequent socio-political unrest. However, a number of the poets associated with Expressionism continued writing in 'Expressionist' ways up to and even beyond 1939, although Expressionism as a general tendency was spent by this time.

It is worth stressing the relations – personal and creative – that existed between poets and artists in the Expressionist years. Lasker-Schüler's poem for George Grosz and Schwitters's piece for Franz Marc give indications of this, and further overlaps with visual art are reflected in the extract from Kokoschka's poem, dedicated to the painter Gustav Klimt, and in Heym's 'The Prisoners I', with its strong evocation of van Gogh's *Prisoners Exercising* (1890; Pushkin Museum, Moscow). *Franz Marc: Postcards to Prince Jussuf,* edited by Peter-Klaus Schuster (Prestel, Munich 1988), is worth mentioning here, as the postcards were for Lasker-Schüler. Wassily Kandinsky's friendships with Franz Marc and Hugo Ball, and Ball's with Hans Arp, are worth noting in this general context too. We should also bear in mind the illustrations of Expressionist poets by artists, for example Ernst Ludwig Kirchner's illustrations of Heym's poetry. As well as this, we would want to emphasise the poems dedicated to other poets, for example Trakl's poem dedicated to Lasker-Schüler and the latter's 'Giselheer' poem for Benn. If space had permitted, we would have included the very moving poem that Lasker-Schüler wrote about Trakl.

The interrelationship between writing and visual art was a striking aspect of German Expressionism, and it is significant to note that a number of Expressionists (and those on the margins of Expressionism) were involved in both visual and textual art forms. We have included work by painter-poets, or artists who also wrote poetry and plays: for instance, Oskar Kokoschka, Max Beckmann, Egon Schiele and Wassily Kandinsky, as well as Hans Arp and Kurt Schwitters. The sculptor Ernst Barlach's Expressionist plays are significant in this regard, too, as are the graphic artist Alfred Kubin's extraordinary novel *Die andere Seite (The Other Side)* and Paul Klee's poetry.

We have included work by twenty eminent translators – poets and scholars – and have tried to establish a good balance of older, well tested translations with new and in some cases previously unpublished ones. Most balances are difficult to achieve and we hope that we have managed to achieve some: undoubtedly poems and translations that could have been included have had to be left out. We'd like to strongly thank all the translators, for the qualities of their work and for the generosity of their time and spirit. It is a simple truth that a book such as this would be impossible without their work and creativity.

Finally, we would like to thank everyone else who has given help with advice and the expediting of final texts, including J.M. Ritchie, Nicholas Jacobs, David Constantine and Anthony Rudolf, and John Jervis, Claire Roberts and all the editorial staff at Tate Publishing.

*David Miller and Stephen Watts*

1. Quoted in Walter H. Sokel's excellent study, *The Writer in Extremis: Expressionism in Twentieth-Century German Literature*, Stanford University Press/McGraw-Hill, 1959/1964, p.51.
2. The title is taken from the poem by Egon Schiele (here included in a translation by Will Stone and Anthony Vivis).
3. In compiling this anthology we have been aware of other anthologies – groundbreaking works such as *Menschheitsdämmerung* edited by Kurt Pinthus (1920; an English translation was published by Camden House in 1994), Michael Hamburger and Christopher Middleton's *Modern German Poetry 1910–1960* (MacGibbon & Kee 1962) and Michael Hamburger's *German Poetry 1910–1975* (Carcanet 1977) – and of the work of

many scholars and translators. At the same time we have followed our own concerns and emphases in the final choice of both texts and translations.
4. A comparison of the Schwitters poems included here with August Stramm's work is highly instructive, both with regard to Stramm's influence on Schwitters and also to Schwitters's distinctively ironic, playful and humorous approach.
5. The artistic responses involve an emphasis on the poet or artist's intense inner or emotional state: this is basic to Expressionism. However, there are widely various approaches to language, imagery and vision involved in poetry (for instance). This can be seen, simply enough, by comparing the poems by Stramm, Stadler, Trakl and Goll, in the present anthology.

# Credits

Every effort has been made to trace the copyright holders of the poems included in this collection. The publishers apologise for any omissions that may inadvertently have been made. The publishers gratefully acknowledge the help of the following for the translations that appear in this volume:

JEREMY ADLER AND BLOOMSBURY for 'Love-Fight' and 'Primal Death' by August Stramm and 'Children in Front of a London Eating-House …' and 'Setting Out' by Ernst Stadler in *The Lost Voices of World War I*, ed. Tim Cross, Bloomsbury 1988

PATRICK BRIDGWATER for 'Rendez-Vous', 'Dream', 'Fickleness', 'Desperate', 'Melancholy', 'Encounter' and 'Fallen' by August Stramm in *August Stramm, twenty two poems*, Brewhouse Press 1969, and 'Screams' and 'Nightscape' by Anton Schnack from *The Journals of Pierre Menard*

MARTIN CHALMERS for 'The Cinema Manager', 'Poem in Prose', 'Ode to Berlin' and 'Underworld' by Ivan Goll. 'The Cinema Manager', 'Ode to Berlin' and 'Underworld' from *Yvan Goll. Die Lyrik in vier Bänden*, hg. u. kommentiert v. Barbara Glauert-Hesse im Auftrag der Fondation Yvan et Claire Goll, Saint-Dié-des-Vosges. © 1996 Argon Verlag Gmbh, Berlin. All rights reserved Wallestein Verlag

Göttingen. 'Poem in Prose' from *Die Aktion: 1911–1918*. Wochenschrift für Politik, Literatur u. Kunst, hrsg. von Franz Pfemfert. Eine Auswahl. Hrsgg.: Thomas Rietzschel. Aufbau-Verl., Berlin u. Weimar. 1986. All rights reserved Wallestein Verlag Göttingen

MICHAEL HAMBURGER for 'On Crossing the Rhine Bridge …' by Ernst Stadler, 'Palau' by Gottfried Benn, 'Decline', 'Occident' and 'Grodek' by Georg Trakl, 'End of the World' by Jakob van Hoddis, and 'Bloodhound' by Ivan Goll in *German Poetry 1910–1975: An Anthology in German and English*, ed. M. Hamburger, Carcanet 1977. From *Gottfried Benn. Sämtliche Werke.* Stuttgarter Ausgabe. Band I: Gedichte I. Klett-Cotta, Stuttgart 1986. © 1986 J. G. Cotta'sche Buchhandlung Nachfolger GmbH, Stuttgart; van Hoddis © Erbengemeinschaft Jakob van Hoddis; and *Yvan Goll. Die Lyrik in vier Bänden*, hg. u. kommentiert v. Barbara Glauert-Hesse im Auftrag der Fondation Yvan et Claire Goll, Saint-Dié-des-Vosges. © 1996 Argon Verlag Gmbh, Berlin. All rights reserved Wallestein Verlag Göttingen

ANTHONY HASLER for 'Last Watch', 'The Prisoners I', 'Berlin I' and 'The Demons of the Cities' by Georg Heym to be published in *Georg Heym: Poems*, Libris 2003

ANSELM HOLLO for 'King Solomon' and 'Waga the Serpent' by Hugo Ball published in the magazine *Collection Four/Tzarad Three*. Translations © 2002 Anselm Hollo

PIERRE JORIS AND UNIVERSITY OF CALIFORNIA PRESS for 'A Bunch of Drifter Sons Hollered' by Gottfried Benn in *Poems for the Millenium: The University of California Book of Modern & Postmodern Poetry* (vol.1), ed. J. Rothenberg and P. Joris, University of California Press 1995. English translation © Pierre Joris. From *Gottfried Benn. Sämtliche Werke*. Stuttgarter Ausgabe. Band I: Gedichte I. Klett-Cotta, Stuttgart 1986. © 1986 J. G. Cotta'sche Buchhandlung Nachfolger GmbH, Stuttgart

PIERRE JORIS AND JEROME ROTHENBERG AND UNIVERSITY OF CALIFORNIA PRESS for 'To the Barbarian:' by Else Lasker-Schüler in *Poems for the Millenium: The University of California Book of Modern & Postmodern Poetry* (vol.1), ed. J. Rothenberg and P. Joris, University of California Press 1995. English translation © Pierre Joris & Jerome Rothenberg

PIERRE JORIS AND EXACT CHANGE for 'Evening' by Kurt Schwitters in Kurt Schwitters, *pppppp: poems performance pieces proses plays poetics*, ed. and tr. Jerome Rothenberg and Pierre Joris, Exact Change 2002

R.J. KAVANAGH for 'Little Aster', 'Happy Youth' and 'Underground Train' by Gottfried Benn in J.M. Ritchie, *Gottfried Benn: The Unreconstructed Expressionist*, Oswald Wolff 1972. From *Gottfried Benn. Sämtliche Werke*. Stuttgarter Ausgabe. Band I: Gedichte 1. Klett-Cotta, Stuttgart 1986. © 1986 J. G. Cotta'sche Buchhandlung Nachfolger GmbH, Stuttgart

ESTHER KINSKY for 'Reconciliation', 'Homesickness', 'To Giselheer the King', 'Oh God', 'The Blue Piano' and 'A Love Song' by Else Lasker-Schüler

R.W. LAST for 'The Bird Plus Three', 'the nightbirds carry…' and 'I am a Horse' by Hans Arp in R.W. Last, *Hans Arp: The poet of Dadaism*, Oswald Wolff 1969

CHRISTOPHER MIDDLETON for 'Georg Grosz' by Else Lasker-Schüler and 'Journey into Misery' by Ivan Goll in *Modern German Poetry 1910–1960: An Anthology*, ed. M. Hamburger and C. Middleton, MacGibbon and Kee 1962. From *Yvan Goll. Die Lyrik in vier Bänden*, hg. u. kommentiert v. Barbara Glauert-Hesse im Auftrag der Fondation Yvan et Claire Goll, Saint-Dié-des-Vosges. © 1996 Argon Verlag Gmbh, Berlin. All rights reserved Wallestein Verlag Göttingen

CHRISTOPHER MIDDLETON for 'Small Town' by Ernst Stadler in *The Lost Voices of World War I*, ed. Tim Cross, Bloomsbury 1988 and for 'Eastern Front' by Georg Trakl in *Georg Trakl. Selected Poems*, Jonathan Cape 1968

CHRISTOPHER MIDDLETON AND CARCANET PRESS for 'The Sun' by Hugo Ball in Christopher Middleton, *Faint Harps and Silver Voices: Selected Translations*, Carcanet Press 2000

MICHAEL MITCHELL AND ARIADNE PRESS for an excerpt from 'The Dreaming Boys' by Oskar Kokoschka from *Oskar Kokoschka: Plays and Poems*, tr. Michael Mitchell, Ariadne Press. English translation © Ariadne Press, Riverside, California

ELIZABETH R. NAPIER AND YALE UNIVERSITY PRESS for 'Still?', 'Sounds' and 'Exit' by Wassily Kandinsky in *Sounds*, Yale University Press 1981

JEROME ROTHENBERG AND EXACT CHANGE for 'Wound Roses Roses Bleed', 'Repose' and 'For Franz Marc' by Kurt Schwitters in Kurt Schwitters, *pppppp: poems performance pieces proses plays poetics*, ed. and trans. Jerome Rothenberg and Pierre Joris, Exact Change 2002

WILL STONE for 'To the Silenced', 'Night', 'To The Boy Elis', and 'De Profundis' by Georg Trakl, first published in 'German and French Poetry', *Modern Poetry in Translation 16*, 2001 and *The Review*, no.6, vol.IV, 2000

WILL STONE AND ANTHONY VIVIS for 'Attack' and 'War Instinct' by August Stramm, and for 'Self Portrait 1 & 2', 'Music while Drowning' and 'Visions' by Egon Schiele in 'European Voices', *Modern Poetry in Translation 18*, 2001 and *Pretext 5*, Spring 2002

ERDMUTE WENZEL WHITE AND CAMDEN HOUSE for 'Cimio' by Hugo Ball in *The Magic Bishop: Hugo Ball, Dada Poet* by Erdmute Wenzel White, Camden House 1998

KEITH WALDROP for 'Summer' and 'Complaint' by Georg Trakl and 'Blue. White. Green.', 'Robespierre' and 'Hunger' by Georg Heym

ROSMARIE WALDROP for 'Jacob' and 'Hagar and Ishmael' by Else Lasker-Schüler in *A Book of Women Poets from Antiquity to Now*, ed. Aliki and Willis Barnstone, Schocken Books 1980, revised ed. 1992

PETER WORTSMAN AND SEAN RAINBIRD for 'Autobiography' by Max Beckmann

# List of illustrated works

Frontispiece: Franz Marc *Black Horse* 1913; Watercolour, gold paper and varnish; Postcard, dated 27 May 1913; Staatliche Museen zu Berlin – Preußischer Kulturbesitz, Kupferstichkabinett/bpk. Photograph: Jörg P. Anders

p.15: Wassily Kandinsky, Illustration for *Klänge*, Munich 1913; Woodcut; By permission the British Library C.106.k.8. © ADAGP, Paris and DACS, London 2003; Photograph: © The British Library

p.21: Erich Heckel *Reading Aloud* 1914; Woodcut; The British Museum, London 1971-2-27-19 © DACS 2003; Photograph: The British Museum, London

p.26: Karl Schmidt-Rottluff *Melancholy* 1914; Woodcut; Staatliche Museen zu Berlin – Preußischer Kulturbesitz, Kupferstichkabinett/bpk. © DACS 2003; Photograph: Jörg P. Anders

p43: Ernst Ludwig Kirchner, Illustration for Georg Heym, *Umbra vitae*, Munich 1924; Woodcut; By permission the British Library C.107.dg.15. © Dr Wolfgang & Ingeborg Henze-Ketterer, Wichtrach/Bern; Photograph: © The British Library

p.48: Karl Schmidt-Rottluff *Stadtbild aus Soest* 1923; Woodcut; Institut für Auslandsbeziehungen e.V., Stuttgart © DACS 2003; Photograph: Hanni Schmitz-Fabri, Cologne

p.52: Hans Arp; Illustration for Richard Huelsenbeck, *Phantastische Gebete*, Zurich 1916; Woodcut; By permission the British Library Cup.408.u.2. © DACS 2003; Photograph: © The British Library

p.59: Max Beckmann *Seduction* 1923; Woodcut; The British Museum, London 1981-7-25-48; © DACS 2003; Photograph: The British Museum, London

p.73: Erich Heckel *Man on a Plain* 1917; Woodcut; The British Museum, London 1982-7-24-19; © DACS 2003; Photograph: The British Museum, London

p.79: Emil Nolde *Prophet* 1912; Woodcut; The British Museum, London 1980-10-11-45 © Dr Manfred Reuther, Siftung Ada und Emil Nolde, Neukirchen; Photograph: The British Museum, London

p.86: Ernst Ludwig Kirchner; Illustration for Alfred Döblin, *Das*

*Stiftsfräulein und der Tod*, Berlin-Wilmersdorf 1913; Woodcut; By permission the British Library C.107.dg.17. ; © Dr Wolfgang & Ingeborg Henze-Ketterer, Wichtrach/Bern; Photograph: © The British Library

p.108: Käthe Kollwitz *Memorial Sheet for Karl Liebknecht* 1920; Woodcut; The British Museum, London 1984-10-6-1 © DACS 2003; Photograph: The British Museum, London